MARIA SHRIVER

A Journey of Strength, Self-Discovery, and the Pursuit of Meaning in a Changing World

By

Morgan A. Ellis

Acknowledgement

I would like to express my deepest gratitude to everyone who
contributed to the creation of this book. Without your support, expertise, and
encouragement, this project would not have been possible.
First and foremost, I want to thank my family for their unwavering belief in me and
their constant encouragement throughout this journey. Your love and support have
been my rock.

I am immensely grateful to my editor, for your keen eye, valuable insights, and
dedication to making this book the best it can be. Your guidance has been invaluable.
To the experts and researchers in the field of fasting and holistic health, I extend my
sincere appreciation for your pioneering work and for sharing your knowledge. Your
contributions have enriched the content of this book.

I would also like to thank my friends and colleagues who provided feedback,
encouragement, and a listening ear when needed. Your enthusiasm for this project kept
me motivated.
Lastly, I extend my gratitude to the readers who have chosen to embark on this
transformative journey with me. Your curiosity and commitment to self-improvement
inspire me, and I hope this book serves as a valuable resource on your path to a happier,
healthier you.
Thank you all for being a part of this transformative process.
With heartfelt appreciation,

Table Of Contents

Prologue

Maria Shriver is not just a journalist, an author, or a former First Lady of California. She is a woman who has spent her life balancing personal challenges with a deep commitment to making the world a better place. She has used her voice, her platform, and her experiences to uplift others, especially women, families, and those affected by Alzheimer's disease.

From the outside, Maria's life might seem like a story of privilege. Born into the Kennedy family, she was surrounded by power, influence, and expectations from an early age. But she has always been clear that privilege does not shield anyone from struggles, nor does it define a person's worth. She has said, "People look at me and see a last name, but what I see is a life full of lessons, heartbreak, and purpose."

One of the most striking things about Maria is her honesty. She has never pretended to be perfect or to have all the answers. In her interviews and speeches, she often shares the challenges she has faced—questioning her purpose, managing personal heartbreak, and finding the courage to start over. She once said, "There have been times when I felt completely lost, when I didn't know what my next step was. But every time, I found my way by focusing on what I could give to the world."

Her journalism career gave her a platform to tell stories that mattered. She didn't just report the news—she focused on issues that were often overlooked, including women's rights, poverty, and healthcare. As a reporter and anchor, she covered stories with depth and empathy, always making sure that the voices of ordinary people were heard. She has said, "It's easy to cover what's loud and dramatic. The harder work is shining a light on what actually changes lives."

Then came her role as the First Lady of California. Maria did not sit on the sidelines. She used her position to advocate for women, education, and families in ways that left a lasting impact. But at the same time, her personal life was unraveling. Her highly publicized split from Arnold Schwarzenegger was one of the most painful moments of her life. Yet, instead of retreating, she chose to face it with grace. She has said, "I learned that endings are not failures. They are opportunities to start again."

Maria has been open about how she found strength in redefining herself. She stepped into a new chapter, using her voice to encourage others to find their own purpose. She became a leading advocate for Alzheimer's research, focusing on the fact that women are disproportionately affected by the disease. She didn't just raise awareness—she pushed for solutions, for funding, for action.

Her books, her speeches, and her work all carry the same message: Life is about meaning, not just success. It's about resilience, not just achievement. She has encouraged people to embrace their struggles, to keep learning, and to never let society define their worth.

Maria Shriver's story is not just one of triumph. It is a story of transformation, of finding purpose in pain, and of using every experience—good or bad—to serve others. As she has said, "You don't have to have it all figured out. You just have to be willing to grow."

This book is about her journey—the challenges she faced, the wisdom she gained, and the impact she continues to make.

Chapter 1

Roots of a Legacy

Maria Shriver was born into one of the most well-known families in American history. She came into the world on November 6, 1955, as a member of the Kennedy family, a name that has been tied to politics, leadership, and public service for generations. Her father, Sargent Shriver, was a respected politician, diplomat, and the first director of the Peace Corps, while her mother, Eunice Kennedy Shriver, was the sister of President John F. Kennedy and the founder of the Special Olympics. From the moment she was born, her life was connected to power, influence, and a strong sense of responsibility to help others.

Maria grew up in a household where leadership was a way of life. Her family wasn't just known for their name—they were known for their actions. The conversations around her weren't about ordinary things. Her parents spoke about changing the world, helping the less fortunate, and fighting for justice. She once shared that she was raised in an environment where "public service wasn't a choice—it was an expectation." That expectation shaped her from a young age.

Her childhood was far from ordinary. While other children played outside without worry, Maria was witnessing history unfold right before her eyes. By the time she was eight years old, her uncle, John F. Kennedy, was the President of the United States. She saw the excitement and energy surrounding his leadership, but she also experienced the deep sorrow that followed his assassination in 1963. That tragedy was the first of many painful losses in her family. Five years later, her uncle, Senator Robert F. Kennedy, was also assassinated. She once described these losses as "life-changing moments that taught me about pain, resilience, and the reality of public life."

Her mother, Eunice, was one of the strongest influences in her life. While Maria's father worked in politics and diplomacy, Eunice was busy creating opportunities for people with disabilities. She founded the Special Olympics, an organization that gave individuals with disabilities a chance to compete, gain confidence, and be recognized for their abilities. Maria has said on multiple occasions that her mother was "relentless, determined, and never took no for an answer." That same determination was instilled in Maria from an early age.

Despite coming from a family that was always in the public eye, Maria was not raised to feel entitled. She was taught to work hard and make a difference. She attended Stone Ridge School of the Sacred Heart, a Catholic all-girls school in Maryland, where discipline and academic excellence were emphasized. Later, she pursued a degree in American Studies at Georgetown University. Education was never just about getting a diploma—it was about understanding history, society, and the responsibility that came with her family name.

Growing up, Maria often struggled with balancing the weight of her legacy with her own identity. She once admitted, "I spent a lot of my early years trying to figure out who I was outside of my family." The world saw her as a Kennedy, but she wanted to be more than just her last name. She was deeply influenced by her mother's passion for service, her father's diplomatic work, and the tragic losses that shaped her family's history. Those experiences created a deep sense of purpose within her.

Maria has always been open about the fact that her family's history was both a gift and a challenge. Being a Kennedy meant that people had high expectations. It meant being under constant public scrutiny. It also meant facing personal hardships on a public stage. She once said, "People assume that coming from a famous family makes everything easier, but that's not always true. Loss, struggle, and pressure don't discriminate."

Despite the challenges, Maria's early years shaped her into the person she would become. She learned that strength comes from purpose, and that making a difference in the world is more important than seeking fame or power. She saw firsthand what leadership looked like—not just in politics, but in service, advocacy, and the way one treats others. Her roots were deeply tied to history, but her path would be one she carved on her own.

Chapter 2

A Kennedy by Birth

Maria Shriver was born into one of the most influential families in American history. From the moment she entered the world on November 6, 1955, in Chicago, Illinois, her last name carried weight. Being a Kennedy meant being part of a family that shaped politics, fought for civil rights, and stood at the center of some of the most significant moments in the country's history. But for Maria, being a Kennedy wasn't just about the legacy—it was about the lessons, the responsibilities, and the expectations that came with it.

Her mother, Eunice Kennedy Shriver, was the sister of President John F. Kennedy and a woman who believed in action over words. She founded the Special Olympics, fought tirelessly for the rights of people with disabilities, and never accepted limitations. Maria has spoken many times about how her mother's influence shaped her, saying, "My mother was tough, determined, and never stopped working. She believed if you saw a problem, you had to fix it."

Her father, Sargent Shriver, was just as dedicated to public service. He wasn't a Kennedy by blood, but he shared the same belief in making a difference. He was the first director of the Peace Corps, helping to build programs that sent young Americans abroad to assist developing nations. Later, he worked in politics and diplomacy, running for Vice President in 1972. His work exposed Maria to the idea that leadership isn't just about speeches—it's about action.

Growing up in the Kennedy family meant that Maria was constantly surrounded by history in the making. She was only three years old when her uncle, John F. Kennedy, was elected President of the United States. She was too young to understand the full impact of his presidency at the time, but she later recalled how the family would gather at the White House, where she would watch her uncle work. She has said, "I was raised to believe that being in public service was a privilege, not a burden."

That privilege came with challenges. Being a Kennedy meant living under intense public scrutiny. When Maria was just eight years old, her uncle John F. Kennedy was assassinated in Dallas, Texas, on November 22, 1963. Five years later, in 1968, her uncle Robert F. Kennedy was also assassinated while running for president. These tragedies didn't just affect her family; they shaped her understanding of the world. She once said, "I learned early on that life isn't fair and that pain doesn't discriminate—even against the most powerful."

Despite the losses, the Kennedys remained committed to their causes. Family gatherings were not just about celebrations—they were about planning the next big initiative, supporting campaigns, and discussing issues that mattered. Public service wasn't a choice in the Kennedy household; it was expected.

Maria has spoken openly about what it was like growing up with a name that carried so much history. She has admitted that it wasn't always easy to balance the expectations that came with being a Kennedy. She once said, "People looked at me and saw a last name before they saw a person. It took me years to step into my own identity."

She attended Stone Ridge School of the Sacred Heart, a Catholic all-girls school in Maryland. There, discipline and academic excellence were expected. Her parents made sure she understood that education was just as important as service. Later, she studied American Studies at Georgetown University, a subject that allowed her to understand the history and political landscape that had shaped her own family's legacy.

But Maria was never just another Kennedy. She was determined to create her own path. She wanted to honor her family's legacy, but she also wanted to find her own voice. She has often spoken about how she spent years trying to prove that she was more than just her last name. She worked hard, pursued journalism, and built a career that was separate from politics. She once said, "I wasn't interested in running for office. I wanted to tell stories. I wanted to give people a voice."

Being a Kennedy by birth meant having opportunities that many didn't. But it also meant carrying the weight of history, the pressure of expectations, and the pain of public loss. Maria Shriver embraced it all—the good, the bad, and the lessons that would shape her into the person she would become.

Chapter 3

Growing Up in the Spotlight

You know, most kids grow up worrying about school, friendships, and what they want to be when they grow up. But Maria Shriver? She grew up with cameras flashing in her face, reporters following her family's every move, and the weight of a famous last name shaping the way the world saw her. Being part of the Kennedy family meant that her childhood was anything but ordinary.

Maria was born on November 6, 1955, into a world where her family's name carried power, influence, and history. Her mother, Eunice Kennedy Shriver, was one of the most determined women in America, pushing for social change and founding the Special Olympics. Her father, Sargent Shriver, was a respected politician and diplomat, deeply involved in public service. Growing up in that kind of environment meant that Maria was always surrounded by discussions about policy, leadership, and making a difference.

She has spoken many times about how her parents raised her with high expectations. Her mother was strict, always pushing her to be independent and resilient. "She never believed in excuses," Maria once said in an interview. "If you had a problem, you figured out how to fix it."

That was the mindset Maria was raised with—always moving forward, always finding solutions. But living under the Kennedy spotlight wasn't easy. The family was admired, but they were also heavily scrutinized. Every move they made was watched, discussed, and analyzed by the public.

Maria attended Stone Ridge School of the Sacred Heart, a private Catholic all-girls school in Maryland. Her parents believed in discipline and structure, and they made sure their children received a strong education. But even at school, Maria couldn't escape her last name. Teachers, classmates, and even strangers treated her differently because she was a Kennedy. People had expectations about who she should be, how she should act, and what path she should take.

Growing up in such a high-profile family also meant dealing with painful public tragedies. Maria was just eight years old when her uncle, President John F. Kennedy, was assassinated in 1963. The entire country mourned, but for Maria, it was personal. She has spoken about how confusing it was to see her family grieving while the whole world was watching.

Then, five years later, in 1968, her uncle Robert F. Kennedy was assassinated while running for president. Another devastating loss. She has said, "Losing two uncles in such violent ways made me realize at a young age that life can change in an instant." Those tragedies forced her to grow up quickly.

Despite the heartbreak, Maria's parents made sure she understood that the family's work had to continue. Public service wasn't just a job for the Kennedys—it was a duty. While other kids were watching cartoons, Maria was listening to conversations about social justice, political campaigns, and world issues. She once shared, "In my house, there was no such thing as small talk. You had to be ready to discuss real issues at the dinner table."

Even though she was surrounded by politics, Maria had different dreams. She wasn't interested in running for office or following in the footsteps of her uncles. What she wanted was to tell stories. She wanted to use her voice in a different way—not through speeches and campaigns, but through journalism.

But breaking away from family expectations wasn't easy. Many people assumed she would stay in politics, and there was always pressure to live up to the Kennedy name.

She later admitted that it took years to step into her own identity. "I spent a lot of time trying to prove that I was more than just my last name," she once said.

Growing up in the public eye meant that every mistake, every decision, and every success was magnified. It meant learning how to navigate a world where people felt they had a right to judge you before they even knew you. But Maria never let the spotlight define her. She took the lessons from her childhood—the discipline, the resilience, and the responsibility—and used them to carve out her own path.

Chapter 4

Lessons from a Powerful Family

When you grow up in a family like Maria Shriver's, lessons aren't just taught—they are lived. The Kennedys weren't just a famous family; they were a family that carried the weight of history on their shoulders. Their name was tied to politics, public service, and tragedy. From a young age, Maria was surrounded by people who shaped the country, and with that came a strong sense of duty.

She has often spoken about how her mother, Eunice Kennedy Shriver, was the biggest influence in her life. Eunice wasn't just another Kennedy sibling—she was a force of nature. She founded the Special Olympics, fought for people with disabilities, and never backed down from a challenge. Maria has said in interviews, "My mother didn't just talk about changing the world—she actually did it." And she expected Maria to do the same.

Eunice was strict. She believed in discipline, hard work, and never making excuses. Maria has said her mother didn't let her sleep in or waste time. "She would wake me up early and tell me to get moving," she once shared. To Eunice, every day was an opportunity to do something meaningful, and she raised her children to believe the same.

Her father, Sargent Shriver, was no different. He helped create the Peace Corps, ran for Vice President, and was known for his kindness and leadership. He taught Maria the importance of treating people with respect, no matter who they were. She once said, "My father was one of the kindest, most optimistic people I've ever met. He always believed in the good in people."

But being part of the Kennedy family wasn't just about learning how to serve—it was about handling pressure. Maria saw firsthand how the public could be harsh, how her family's successes were celebrated, but their failures were picked apart. She learned that criticism was part of the deal. If you were a Kennedy, you had to be tough.

She also learned about loss. Her uncles, President John F. Kennedy and Robert F. Kennedy, were assassinated when she was a child. She once said, "I learned early on that life can change in an instant. My family had to keep going, no matter what." The tragedies didn't break them; they strengthened their belief in service and purpose.

But even with all these lessons, Maria wanted something different. Many expected her to go into politics, but she had other plans. She was drawn to storytelling, to journalism. She wanted to ask questions, to report on real issues, and to connect with people outside of politics. "I knew I wanted to use my voice, but in my own way," she said in an interview.

Maria's journey wasn't about escaping her family's legacy—it was about building her own. The lessons she learned from her parents and uncles stayed with her, shaping the way she approached her career and personal life. Hard work, service, resilience—those were the values she carried forward. And as she stepped into the world of journalism, she brought those lessons with her, proving that being a Kennedy was not just about where you came from, but what you did with it.

Chapter 5

The Influence of Her Parents

Maria Shriver was never just another Kennedy. She was raised with a deep sense of responsibility, and that came directly from her parents, Eunice Kennedy Shriver and Sargent Shriver. They weren't just well-known figures; they were individuals who dedicated their lives to making a difference. Their influence shaped Maria in ways she has openly discussed throughout her life.

Her mother, Eunice, was a powerhouse. She had a relentless drive to help those in need, particularly people with intellectual disabilities. She founded the Special Olympics, an organization that has since changed millions of lives. Maria has spoken many times about her mother's passion and discipline, saying, "She didn't believe in wasting time. If you weren't doing something useful, she would find something for you to do."

Eunice expected excellence. Maria grew up watching her mother work tirelessly, often making phone calls at the kitchen table, organizing events, and demanding action from world leaders. There was no room for self-pity or laziness in the Shriver household. Maria once recalled, "My mother never coddled us. If we wanted something, we had to work for it." That mindset pushed Maria to work hard in school, pursue her dreams, and stay focused on her goals.

Sargent Shriver, Maria's father, was different but just as impactful. He was known for his optimism and kindness. He helped create the Peace Corps and led anti-poverty programs that changed the lives of countless Americans. While Eunice was tough and determined, Sargent was compassionate and deeply caring. Maria has often said, "My father was the most hopeful person I ever knew. He believed in the power of good."

Unlike her mother, who pushed hard, Sargent led by example. He treated everyone with respect, from world leaders to the people he met on the street. Maria once shared a story about how her father would stop and talk to strangers, genuinely interested in their lives. "He taught me that everyone has a story worth listening to," she said. That lesson stayed with her as she pursued journalism, always looking for the human side of every story.

Maria's parents had high expectations, but they also gave her a strong foundation of values. Public service, faith, hard work—these weren't just words in the Shriver household. They were a way of life. Maria saw firsthand what it meant to dedicate yourself to others. She grew up understanding that success wasn't about personal gain, but about how much you could give back.

At times, it wasn't easy. Being the daughter of such powerful figures meant there was always pressure to live up to their standards. Maria has admitted, "For a long time, I struggled with the idea that I had to be just like my parents." But instead of following directly in their footsteps, she chose her own path—one that still honored their legacy, but in a way that felt right for her.

Their influence never faded. Even as Maria built her career, raised her family, and faced life's challenges, the lessons from her parents stayed with her. She carried her mother's determination and her father's kindness, blending them into a life that was uniquely her own.

Chapter 6

Shaping Her Own Identity

Maria Shriver was born into a world where expectations were set before she could walk. Being a Kennedy by blood and a Shriver by name meant she was constantly compared to the powerful figures in her family. But Maria never wanted to be defined solely by her last name. She wanted to carve her own path, and she worked relentlessly to make that happen.

From a young age, she knew she wasn't just the daughter of Eunice Kennedy Shriver and Sargent Shriver—she was an individual with her own voice, dreams, and ambitions. She has spoken openly about the challenges of growing up in such a high-profile family, saying, "People always asked me if I was going to run for office like my uncles, but I wanted to find my own way."

Journalism became her way of doing just that. While politics was the natural route for many in her family, Maria was drawn to storytelling. She wanted to be the one asking the questions, shining a light on important issues, and giving a voice to those who weren't always heard. She studied American Studies at Georgetown University, then went on to build a career in broadcast journalism, proving that she was more than just her famous last name.

Her early years in television weren't easy. She had to prove herself in a field that wasn't always welcoming to women, let alone one carrying the weight of such a well-known family. Maria worked for CBS Morning News and later became a co-anchor for NBC's Sunday Today. She was committed to delivering serious news, not just being a name on the screen. "I didn't want to be given a job because of my family. I wanted to earn it," she once said.

She did more than just earn it—she excelled. Maria became an award-winning journalist, covering major political events, interviewing world leaders, and reporting on stories that mattered. But she never lost sight of what made her unique. Unlike many reporters who chased headlines, Maria focused on human stories. She wanted people to feel seen, to feel heard.

Even as she built her career, she was constantly balancing her personal life. She married Arnold Schwarzenegger, a man who was a celebrity in his own right. For years, she supported his ambitions while maintaining her own. When he became Governor of California, Maria took on the role of First Lady, using her platform to advocate for women, Alzheimer's awareness, and children's issues. But even then, she didn't let that role define her.

Maria has said, "Being a wife, a mother, a journalist—these are all parts of me. But at the end of the day, I have to ask myself, 'Who am I outside of all these roles?'" That question became even more important when her marriage ended. Divorce is never easy, but going through it in the public eye made it even more challenging. Still, she found strength in rediscovering who she was.

In recent years, Maria has focused on personal growth and helping others do the same. She has written books about life transitions, hosted conversations on The Sunday Paper, and spoken about the importance of self-reflection. She reminds people that it's okay to evolve, to change direction, and to embrace new seasons in life.

Maria Shriver didn't follow the script written for her. She wrote her own. And in doing so, she has shown the world that identity isn't about where you come from—it's about who you choose to become.

Chapter 7

Finding Her Voice in Journalism

Maria Shriver didn't step into journalism because it was easy. She did it because she had something to say. Unlike many in her family, she wasn't drawn to politics. She wanted to ask tough questions, bring important stories to light, and give people a voice.

She studied American Studies at Georgetown University, but her true education began when she entered the world of broadcast journalism. It wasn't a glamorous start. She worked hard behind the scenes, learning the craft before ever appearing on camera. Maria knew that carrying the Kennedy name meant people would question if she had earned her place. She made sure there was no doubt.

Her first big break came when she joined CBS Morning News as a writer and producer. She wasn't just handed the job—she worked her way up, proving herself with every story she covered. From there, she moved to NBC News, where she became a co-anchor for Sunday Today. She covered politics, world events, and human-interest stories, showing a deep curiosity and respect for the people she interviewed.

Maria has always said she wasn't interested in the kind of journalism that focused on scandal or gossip. "I wanted to tell stories that made a difference, that helped people understand the world and themselves a little better," she once shared in an interview. That commitment set her apart.

She didn't just sit behind a desk. She traveled, reported from the field, and covered some of the most defining moments in history. She interviewed world leaders, reported on presidential elections, and gave a platform to voices that were often ignored. She won a Peabody Award for her work on women's health issues and became known for bringing depth and empathy to every story she covered.

Maria also understood that journalism wasn't just about delivering the news—it was about shaping conversations. She spent years as a Dateline NBC correspondent, diving into stories that mattered. But her work wasn't just about informing the public. It was about challenging them to care.

Even as her career flourished, Maria faced challenges. She was balancing her personal life, raising a family, and supporting her husband, Arnold Schwarzenegger, through his Hollywood career and political ambitions. When he became Governor of California, Maria stepped back from journalism to focus on her role as First Lady. But even then, she found ways to continue meaningful work. She launched The Women's Conference, bringing together powerful voices to discuss leadership, empowerment, and change.

When her marriage ended, Maria found herself at a crossroads. She was no longer a journalist in the traditional sense, but she never lost her voice. Instead, she redefined what journalism could be. She started The Sunday Paper, a digital newsletter focused on personal growth, community, and purpose-driven storytelling. She wrote bestselling books, gave speeches, and used her platform to discuss issues like Alzheimer's awareness, mental health, and faith.

Maria Shriver never let anyone define what her career should look like. She built it on her own terms, using her voice to inspire, inform, and uplift. And after decades in journalism, she is still doing exactly that.

Chapter 8

Love, Marriage, and Public Scrutiny

Maria Shriver's relationship with Arnold Schwarzenegger was never just a private matter.
From the moment they got together, the world watched closely. She was a Kennedy,
raised in a family where politics and legacy shaped everything. He was a bodybuilding
champion turned Hollywood action star, an outsider to the world of American politics.
To many, they seemed like opposites. But Maria always said their relationship was built
on love, respect, and a shared desire to push boundaries.

She met Arnold in 1977 at a charity event, introduced by Tom Brokaw. At the time, she
was already making her mark in journalism, while Arnold was still building his
Hollywood career. Their connection was instant, but their relationship wasn't rushed.
They dated for nearly nine years before finally getting married in 1986 in a grand
ceremony at the Kennedy family estate in Massachusetts.

Marriage to Arnold wasn't just about love. It also meant navigating intense public
attention. Maria, who grew up in a politically powerful family, was used to the spotlight,
but Arnold's level of fame introduced a new dynamic. The media followed their every
move, and their marriage was often a topic of speculation. People questioned how a
Kennedy and a movie star could make it work, but Maria always stood by her husband.

She once said, "I didn't marry Arnold because he was a movie star. I married him because
I loved him, because he made me laugh, and because I believed in his dreams as much as
he believed in mine."

For years, they balanced two high-profile careers and raised their four
children—Katherine, Christina, Patrick, and Christopher—with a strong emphasis on

family values. Maria was always protective of her children, ensuring they had as normal a life as possible despite their parents' fame.

When Arnold decided to run for Governor of California in 2003, Maria faced one of the biggest shifts in her life. She had spent decades building her career in journalism, but she put it on hold to support him. Becoming the First Lady of California was a role she never planned for, but she embraced it. She used her platform to advocate for women's rights, Alzheimer's awareness, and social programs, proving she was much more than just "the governor's wife."

But as the public watched their successes, they also speculated about their struggles. In 2011, Maria and Arnold announced their separation after 25 years of marriage, and soon after, the truth came out—Arnold had fathered a child with their housekeeper. The revelation was devastating, not just because of the betrayal but because it played out in the public eye.

Maria later spoke about how painful the experience was. She said, "This is a painful and heartbreaking time. As a mother, my concern is for the children. I ask for compassion, respect, and privacy as my children and I try to rebuild our lives."

Despite everything, she handled the situation with grace. She didn't speak badly about Arnold, even when she had every reason to. She focused on healing, moving forward, and redefining herself outside of the marriage.

Maria's story isn't just about a relationship that ended—it's about resilience. She built a new life, found her own voice again, and continued her work in journalism, advocacy, and writing. Even after the divorce, she and Arnold maintained a relationship of mutual respect for the sake of their children. She once said, "No matter what happens, we are still a family, and we will always support each other."

Maria Shriver never let her marriage define her. She loved, she lost, but she never lost herself.

Chapter 9

The Role of First Lady of California

Maria Shriver never planned to become the First Lady of California. She had spent years building a respected career in journalism, working for major networks and earning awards for her reporting. But in 2003, everything changed when her husband, Arnold Schwarzenegger, announced he was running for Governor of California. That decision placed Maria in a position she never expected, and once again, she had to redefine her life.

At first, she wasn't sure how she felt about the role. She had grown up in politics, being the niece of President John F. Kennedy and the daughter of Sargent Shriver, the founding director of the Peace Corps. She knew how political life could take a toll on a family. But when Arnold won the election, she decided she would not be a traditional First Lady—she would create her own path.

She once said, "I wanted to use my platform to shine a light on people who didn't always have a voice. That was my mission."

From the beginning, Maria made it clear she wasn't just going to host ceremonial events and smile for the cameras. She focused on causes that mattered to her, like women's empowerment, Alzheimer's awareness, and social justice. She launched the We Connect initiative, which helped low-income families access education, healthcare, and financial resources. She worked on The Women's Conference, turning it into one of the most influential gatherings for women's leadership in the country.

Maria also led efforts to support caregivers and families affected by Alzheimer's disease, something deeply personal to her because of her father's battle with the illness. She didn't just talk about the issue—she took action, pushing for research funding and speaking openly about the emotional toll of caregiving.

Being First Lady meant balancing her public role with her private struggles. While she was leading statewide programs and advocating for change, she was also managing the challenges of her marriage, raising four children, and adjusting to a life where her every move was scrutinized. But she handled it all with grace, refusing to let politics change who she was.

She later reflected on her time in Sacramento, saying, "I had to figure out how to be Maria in the middle of it all. I was not just 'the governor's wife'—I was a mother, a journalist, and an advocate. That's how I led."

Maria Shriver left a lasting impact as First Lady. She wasn't just a supporting figure—she was a leader in her own right. Even after Arnold's time in office ended, she continued the work she had started, proving that the title was never what mattered. What mattered was using her voice to make a difference.

Chapter 10

Balancing Career and Family

Maria Shriver has always been clear about one thing—she never wanted to be defined by just one role. She was a journalist, a mother, a wife, an advocate, and a public figure, all at the same time. But balancing those responsibilities was never easy, and she has been open about the challenges that came with it.

She built her career in journalism at a young age, working hard to establish her own name outside of her famous family. She worked for CBS News, then became a correspondent for Dateline NBC, where she covered major stories around the world. She won Peabody and Emmy awards for her reporting, proving that she was more than just the niece of a president or the daughter of a political icon. She had her own voice and a deep passion for storytelling.

At the same time, Maria was also a mother of four—Katherine, Christina, Patrick, and Christopher—and raising a family while maintaining a demanding career was never simple. She once said, "People would ask me, 'How do you do it all?' And the truth is, I didn't. Some days I was great at my job, and some days I was great at being a mom. But I never felt like I was doing everything perfectly at the same time."

Her role changed drastically when her husband, Arnold Schwarzenegger, became Governor of California in 2003. She had to leave her job at NBC due to conflicts of interest, and for the first time in her career, she was no longer working as a journalist. That shift was difficult for her. She had always prided herself on being independent, and suddenly, she found herself in a supporting role instead of leading her own career.

But Maria didn't let that stop her from making an impact. She used her platform as First Lady of California to launch The Women's Conference, expanding it into one of the most powerful gatherings for women's leadership. She created the We Connect program, helping families in need. She advocated for Alzheimer's awareness, inspired by her father's battle with the disease. She found ways to continue working on issues she cared about, even when she wasn't officially in the media.

When her marriage ended, Maria had to rebuild her life again. She has said openly, "I had to ask myself, 'Who am I now? What do I want my life to look like?'" She returned to journalism, writing books and creating content that focused on empowerment, personal growth, and faith. She started producing documentaries about mental health and caregiving, proving that her storytelling ability was still strong.

Balancing career and family was never easy for Maria Shriver, and she has never pretended that it was. She has talked about the guilt that working mothers feel, the pressure of trying to do it all, and the importance of forgiving yourself when things don't go perfectly. But through all the challenges, she never gave up on her passions or her family. She found ways to adapt, evolve, and keep moving forward. That, more than anything, is what defines her journey.

Chapter 11

Challenges Behind the Scenes

Maria Shriver's life has always looked polished on the outside. She came from a legendary political family, built a successful career in journalism, married a world-famous actor, and became the First Lady of California. But behind the scenes, she faced struggles that tested her strength, her values, and her identity.

She has spoken openly about feeling like she never fully belonged in any one role. Growing up as a Kennedy, she was expected to follow in the footsteps of her family's legacy of public service. But she was drawn to journalism, where she worked hard to make a name for herself separate from her famous relatives. Even when she became a respected reporter, some still viewed her as just "a Kennedy," which made it difficult to prove herself purely on her own merit.

Balancing personal life and professional ambitions was another challenge. Maria had four children while building her career at CBS News and NBC. She worked long hours, traveled frequently, and covered serious global issues, but she also wanted to be fully present as a mother. She has admitted, "I always felt torn. If I was at work, I felt guilty about not being home. If I was home, I felt guilty about not working."

The biggest public challenge of her life came in 2011 when her marriage to Arnold Schwarzenegger ended after 25 years. The world learned that Arnold had fathered a child with their longtime housekeeper, and suddenly, Maria's personal pain became front-page news. The betrayal was devastating, not just because of the marriage, but because family had always been at the center of her identity. She has said, "I was completely lost. I had built my life around being a wife and a mother, and I didn't know what my future looked like."

Instead of hiding, Maria used the experience to redefine herself. She stepped away from public life for a while, focusing on her children and personal healing. She turned to her faith and therapy, seeking guidance on how to rebuild. In interviews, she has spoken about learning to stand on her own again, saying, "I had spent my whole life being part of something bigger—part of a family, part of a marriage. I had to figure out who I was on my own."

Her father's battle with Alzheimer's disease was another deeply personal struggle. Watching Sargent Shriver suffer from memory loss was heartbreaking, and Maria became a strong advocate for Alzheimer's awareness. She dedicated time to educating people about the disease, pushing for research, and supporting caregivers. Even in her grief, she turned pain into purpose.

Maria has never claimed to have a perfect life. She has been honest about her mistakes, her fears, and the moments when she felt like everything was falling apart. But no matter how many challenges she faced, she kept moving forward, using every difficulty as a chance to grow, learn, and help others. That resilience is what has always defined her—not just the success people see on the surface, but the battles she fought behind the scenes.

Chapter 12

Heartbreak and Personal Transformation

Maria Shriver has lived a life in the public eye, but no amount of fame, power, or family legacy could shield her from heartbreak. When her marriage to Arnold Schwarzenegger ended, the world watched as her private pain became headline news. She was not just dealing with the collapse of a 25-year marriage; she was rebuilding her entire identity.

She has spoken about the deep sense of loss she felt. "I had built my life around my marriage and my family. When it all fell apart, I didn't know who I was outside of that." For years, she had played the role of a devoted wife, a mother of four, and a political partner. Now, she had to navigate life on her own.

Divorce is painful for anyone, but for Maria, the betrayal was made worse by the relentless media coverage. She could not grieve in private. Every detail was analyzed, every emotion scrutinized. People debated how she should respond, how she should heal. But Maria refused to let others define her journey. She took a step back from the public eye, choosing to heal on her own terms.

One of the first things she did was turn inward. She sought therapy, leaned on her faith, and took long walks to clear her mind. She has said, "I had to quiet the noise around me so I could hear my own voice again." For years, she had been a part of something bigger—a marriage, a political dynasty, a well-known family. Now, she had to figure out who she was when all of that was stripped away.

She focused on her own growth, stepping into new opportunities that were fully hers. She returned to journalism, writing and speaking about issues that mattered deeply to her. She also became an advocate for women going through personal reinvention, reminding them that life does not end after heartbreak. "So many women come up to me and say, 'I don't know who I am anymore.' And I tell them, 'That's okay. You get to figure it out now. You get to build something new.'"

Another major transformation in her life was her focus on mental health and self-care. Maria had spent years taking care of others—her husband, her children, her parents. But for the first time, she prioritized herself. She openly spoke about the pressure women face to be everything for everyone and how damaging that can be. "We're told to hold everything together, to never break. But the truth is, we all break sometimes. And it's in that breaking that we find out who we really are."

Maria's heartbreak did not break her. It reshaped her. She emerged as a woman who was no longer defined by her last name, her marriage, or her role in someone else's life. She became the author of her own story, proving that personal transformation is possible at any stage of life. "I am not the same woman I was ten years ago. And I don't want to be. I have grown, I have changed, and I have learned that my life is fully my own."

Maria's journey through heartbreak was not just about loss; it was about discovering her strength, her purpose, and her ability to stand tall on her own. She did not let pain define her. Instead, she used it to create something new—a life that was fully, unapologetically hers.

Chapter 13

Her Journey Through Healing

Maria Shriver has always been a woman of strength, but even the strongest people need time to heal. After facing personal and public challenges, she made a decision—she would not let heartbreak or pain define her. Instead, she would focus on healing, rebuilding, and stepping into the next phase of her life with purpose.

She has spoken openly about how difficult it was to face life after her marriage ended. For years, she had been a wife, a political partner, and a public figure linked to one of the most famous families in America. When all of that changed, she felt lost. "I had to figure out who I was without the labels. That was terrifying, but also freeing."

Her healing process was not rushed. Maria gave herself the space to grieve, reflect, and grow. She turned to therapy, something she has encouraged others to do, calling it "one of the most powerful tools for self-discovery." She also deepened her faith, often speaking about how prayer and meditation became central to her healing.

One of the biggest lessons she learned was about letting go of expectations. She had always been someone who carried the weight of responsibility—raising a family, supporting a husband in politics, and maintaining a career. But through her healing journey, she realized that it was okay to put herself first. She has said, "Women are taught to take care of everyone else first. But you can't pour from an empty cup. I had to learn to take care of myself."

She also turned to physical wellness as part of her healing. She embraced exercise, making long walks a part of her daily routine. She spoke about the importance of movement, saying that it helped clear her mind and reset her emotions.

Maria also found healing in her work. She returned to journalism with a new sense of purpose, focusing on issues that mattered deeply to her—women's empowerment, aging, and mental health. She launched initiatives that encouraged women to embrace personal transformation at any stage of life. She has said, "You are never too old, too late, or too broken to start over."

She didn't just focus on healing herself—she used her journey to help others heal. She created spaces where people could openly discuss their struggles without shame. She emphasized compassion, understanding, and the importance of lifting each other up.

Through her healing, Maria became a new version of herself—one that was not defined by her past but shaped by her experiences. She emerged not just as a survivor of hardship, but as a woman who had reclaimed her life on her own terms. "I am still learning, still evolving, and still finding my way. And that's okay. Life is not about having all the answers; it's about giving yourself the grace to grow."

Her journey through healing was not just about moving on. It was about becoming whole again. And in that process, she has inspired countless others to do the same.

Chapter 14

The Fight for Alzheimer's Awareness

Maria Shriver's fight against Alzheimer's disease is deeply personal. When her father, Sargent Shriver, was diagnosed with the disease, she didn't just watch from the sidelines—she stepped up and became one of the most vocal advocates in the country. She has often spoken about how heartbreaking it was to see her father, a man known for his intelligence and leadership, slowly lose his memory. "Alzheimer's doesn't just take the person you love," she has said. "It takes them little by little, right in front of your eyes."

This fight became her mission. She didn't want other families to go through the same pain without support, resources, and, most importantly, hope. That's why she launched The Women's Alzheimer's Movement (WAM), a groundbreaking organization focused on raising awareness, funding research, and advocating for policy changes.

Maria has always highlighted the fact that Alzheimer's affects women at a much higher rate than men. Two-thirds of those diagnosed with the disease are women, and women are also more likely to be caregivers for loved ones suffering from it. She has called this "a women's health crisis that no one is talking about." Through WAM, she has worked to educate women about brain health, early detection, and lifestyle changes that can reduce the risk of developing the disease.

Her work didn't stop with advocacy. She used her platform as a journalist to spread awareness on a national level. She produced "The Alzheimer's Project," an Emmy-winning documentary series that aired on HBO. It gave viewers a close look at the impact of the disease—not just on patients, but on families and caregivers. She also wrote "The Shriver Report: A Woman's Nation Takes on Alzheimer's," a major study that revealed how Alzheimer's disproportionately affects women.

Maria's passion for this cause has taken her to Congress, the White House, and medical research centers. She has pushed for more funding, better support for caregivers, and greater public awareness. She has said, "This disease is not just about getting old. It's about all of us. And we need to act now."

She has also made brain health a key part of her message. Through her books, interviews, and speeches, she has encouraged people to focus on exercise, healthy eating, stress reduction, and lifelong learning to keep their minds strong. She has worked with scientists, doctors, and health organizations to make sure people have the information they need to take control of their brain health before it's too late.

Her efforts have made a real difference. She has helped raise millions of dollars for research, and her advocacy has pushed Alzheimer's into the national conversation. She is not just talking about change—she is creating it.

Maria has often said that her father's battle with Alzheimer's changed her. It made her more determined, more compassionate, and more committed to making an impact. "My father may have lost his memory, but he never lost his heart," she once said. That same heart drives Maria's fight today, as she continues working to find a cure, support families, and ensure that no one faces this disease alone.

Chapter 15

Faith, Purpose, and Personal Growth

Maria Shriver has always been open about the role faith plays in her life. It has been her foundation through moments of joy, heartbreak, uncertainty, and transformation. She was raised in a deeply Catholic household, where faith wasn't just something practiced on Sundays—it was a guiding principle for how to live. Her mother, Eunice Kennedy Shriver, was a woman of deep conviction, and her father, Sargent Shriver, often leaned on prayer in times of difficulty. That sense of belief stayed with Maria throughout her life, even as she faced challenges that tested her strength.

She has spoken many times about how faith helped her through some of her most difficult moments. When her marriage to Arnold Schwarzenegger ended, she turned to prayer and self-reflection to help her heal. She once said, "When you've spent your life defining yourself in relation to someone else, it's a real awakening to suddenly have to stand on your own." That period of loss and rediscovery led her to ask deeper questions: Who am I outside of my roles? What truly gives my life meaning?

Maria has always been a seeker. She doesn't claim to have all the answers, but she constantly searches for truth, whether through faith, learning, or meaningful conversations. She has interviewed religious leaders, scientists, and everyday people who have faced adversity, all in an effort to understand the human spirit. Her curiosity and willingness to grow have shaped her into the woman she is today.

One of the ways Maria channels her faith and purpose is through her writing. She has authored books like I've Been Thinking...: Reflections, Prayers, and Meditations for a Meaningful Life, where she shares personal stories, prayers, and wisdom she has gathered over the years. She wants to help people find peace in their struggles and purpose in their pain. She has said, "You don't have to have it all figured out. Life is about evolving, forgiving yourself, and moving forward with faith."

Another major part of her journey has been learning to let go of outside expectations. For years, she lived in the public eye as a journalist, a first lady of California, and a member of the Kennedy family. With those roles came pressure—pressure to be perfect, to meet everyone's expectations, to never show vulnerability. But as she has gotten older, she has embraced a different mindset. "I no longer chase the idea of being perfect," she has said. "I just want to be real, to be true to myself, and to live with purpose."

That sense of purpose extends to her work in philanthropy and advocacy. Whether she's fighting for Alzheimer's awareness, supporting women's empowerment, or helping people strengthen their faith, Maria is always focused on making a difference. She believes that true fulfillment comes not from material success, but from serving others, staying curious, and being open to change.

Maria often encourages people to slow down and listen—to themselves, to their faith, and to the wisdom that life is constantly offering. She has said that one of the most important lessons she has learned is that growth never stops. No matter what stage of life you're in, there's always room to deepen your faith, find new purpose, and become a better version of yourself.

Her journey is not about having all the answers—it's about staying open, trusting the process, and believing that every experience, no matter how difficult, is shaping you into who you're meant to be. Maria Shriver's life is proof that faith, purpose, and personal growth are not destinations. They are lifelong commitments.

Chapter 16

Hidden Struggles and Inner Strength

Maria Shriver has always been in the public eye, but few people truly understand the personal battles she has faced behind closed doors. She was born into the Kennedy family, one of the most famous and scrutinized families in American history. From a young age, there were expectations—she was expected to carry the family's legacy, to work hard, to give back, and to always present a composed, graceful image. But like anyone else, she has had her share of struggles.

She has spoken about how difficult it was to constantly prove herself. Being a Kennedy meant being part of something bigger than yourself, but it also meant living under constant public judgment. She once said, "When you grow up in a family like mine, you learn early on that people have a vision for your life before you even get a chance to figure it out yourself." That pressure was real, and while it gave her a sense of purpose, it also made her question where her true identity fit into it all.

Her career as a journalist was one way she tried to carve out her own path. She worked hard to be recognized for her intelligence and abilities, not just her last name. She became an Emmy-winning journalist, an anchor, and a respected voice in media. Yet, even as she succeeded professionally, she often felt pulled in different directions—between her career, her role as a mother, and her responsibilities as the First Lady of California. There were moments of exhaustion, moments of self-doubt, moments where she questioned whether she was doing enough or if she was even on the right path.

One of the hardest struggles Maria has ever faced was the collapse of her marriage to Arnold Schwarzenegger. After 25 years together, she was blindsided by the revelation that he had fathered a child with their longtime housekeeper. The betrayal was devastating. She has openly said that the divorce forced her to completely reevaluate her life. She described it as a moment where everything she had built—her family, her home, her sense of stability—suddenly crumbled. "I had to stand alone for the first time in my life," she said. "I had to figure out who I was without all the roles I had played for so long."

Maria struggled with the pain privately while the world speculated publicly. Tabloids ran endless headlines, but she remained silent, choosing to focus on healing rather than fueling media drama. She leaned on her faith, her children, and her close friends to get through it. Instead of allowing heartbreak to define her, she used it as an opportunity to grow. She returned to her writing, putting her emotions into words, hoping that her story could help others going through their own struggles.

She also had to battle moments of self-doubt about aging. For a long time, she struggled with the idea of getting older, particularly after years of being in front of cameras. But over time, she began to see aging not as something to fear, but as a chance to evolve. She once said, "I don't want to spend my life worrying about wrinkles. I want to spend it learning, helping, and being present for the people I love."

Through all of her hidden struggles, one thing has remained constant—her inner strength. Maria never let pain defeat her. She turned every challenge into a lesson, every hardship into an opportunity to grow. She has used her voice to uplift others, reminding people that struggle does not make you weak—it makes you human. And in that humanity, there is strength.

Chapter 17

Her Impact on Women's Empowerment

Maria Shriver has spent decades lifting up women, giving them a voice, and encouraging them to embrace their power. She has never been someone who just talks about empowerment—she has actively worked to create change. From her journalism career to her advocacy work, she has made it clear that women deserve equal opportunities, respect, and a platform to share their stories.

She has often spoken about how her upbringing shaped her views on women's empowerment. Growing up in the Kennedy family, she saw firsthand how strong, intelligent women could influence the world. Her mother, Eunice Kennedy Shriver, founded the Special Olympics and never let obstacles stand in her way. Maria saw that strength in action and carried it into her own life. She once said, "I was raised to believe that if you have a voice, you should use it. If you have a platform, you should lift others up."

Her time as a journalist gave her a front-row seat to the challenges women face. She covered stories about women breaking barriers, but she also saw how much work still needed to be done. Whether she was reporting on single mothers struggling to make ends meet, women fighting for leadership roles, or survivors of domestic violence, she used her platform to bring attention to issues that often went unnoticed.

Maria didn't just report on these issues—she took action. She launched The Shriver Report, a groundbreaking project that studied the economic challenges women face in the United States. She gathered research, interviewed real women, and exposed the truth: women were working just as hard as men, yet they were still being undervalued and underpaid. Her work forced policymakers and business leaders to confront these realities.

She has also been a strong advocate for working mothers. As a mother of four, she knows the pressures of balancing career and family. She has spoken about the guilt that many women feel when trying to juggle both. She once said, "Women are constantly being told they have to do it all, but we need to change that narrative. Women don't have to do it all—they just need support."

During her time as First Lady of California, she championed programs that helped women find jobs, gain financial independence, and access education. She didn't just make speeches—she pushed for real policy changes. She also used her influence to promote self-care and mental well-being, reminding women that their worth is not just tied to their work or family roles.

Maria has also been vocal about the need for women to support one another. She has spoken about the pressures society places on women to compete, but she believes true empowerment comes from lifting each other up. She encourages women to mentor, encourage, and create opportunities for one another rather than tearing each other down.

Her impact goes beyond speeches and reports. She has personally mentored young women, provided scholarships, and helped women tell their stories through her books and media projects. Whether she's speaking on television, writing a book, or creating a new initiative, her message remains the same: women are powerful, capable, and worthy of every opportunity.

Maria Shriver's work in women's empowerment is not just about policy changes or statistics—it's about real lives. She has helped countless women find their strength, believe in themselves, and fight for their place in the world. Her voice has made a difference, and her actions have left a lasting mark.

Chapter 18

Reflections on Life and Legacy

Maria Shriver has spent her life questioning what truly matters. She has openly shared her struggles, triumphs, and lessons, hoping that others can find meaning in their own journeys. Her legacy is not just about what she has accomplished—it's about the impact she has had on others and the wisdom she has gained along the way.

She often speaks about the importance of self-reflection. Maria has said that people spend so much time chasing success, approval, and external validation, but at the end of the day, what truly matters is inner peace and personal fulfillment. She encourages people to slow down, take a step back, and ask themselves what kind of life they want to live.

One of the biggest lessons she has shared is the value of resilience. She has faced public scrutiny, personal heartbreak, and professional challenges, but she has always found a way to keep moving forward. She once said, "I have fallen many times, but every time, I got up. And every time I got up, I learned something new about myself."

Maria's reflections on family are just as powerful. She has spoken about the deep influence of her parents, especially her mother, Eunice Kennedy Shriver, who showed her what it means to serve others. She has also expressed gratitude for her children, saying that they have been her greatest teachers. "My kids remind me every day that love, kindness, and honesty matter more than any title or achievement."

She has also reflected on her work as a journalist and advocate. Through her writing, reporting, and public service, she has always tried to shine a light on the issues that matter most. But she acknowledges that real change takes time. She has said, "Progress is slow, and sometimes it feels like we're not moving forward at all. But if you keep pushing, keep speaking up, and keep believing, things do change."

Faith has played a major role in Maria's journey. She often talks about how her spiritual beliefs have helped her find strength in difficult moments. She believes that life is not just about personal success but about using one's gifts to serve others. She has said, "We are all here for a reason. We all have something to contribute. The challenge is figuring out what that is and having the courage to pursue it."

As Maria looks back on her life, she doesn't just focus on achievements—she focuses on the people she has helped, the lives she has touched, and the lessons she has learned. She wants her legacy to be one of kindness, courage, and service. She has often said that the greatest measure of a life is not wealth or fame but the love and impact one leaves behind.

Maria Shriver's story is far from over. She continues to inspire, challenge, and encourage people to live with purpose. And as she reflects on her journey, one message remains clear: life is not about perfection—it's about growth, love, and making a difference.

Chapter 19

Lessons from Triumphs and Setbacks

Maria Shriver has never been afraid to talk about the highs and lows of her life. She has been open about her triumphs, but she has also shared the painful lessons that came from her setbacks. Whether in her career, personal life, or advocacy work, she has always believed that every experience holds something valuable.

One of the biggest lessons she has shared is about resilience. Maria has said many times that life doesn't always go the way you expect, but what matters is how you respond. She once said, "Failure is not the end of the story—it's just another chapter." When she faced personal struggles, including the public breakdown of her marriage, she didn't hide. She took time to reflect, to heal, and to rebuild her life in a way that felt true to who she was.

Her professional journey has also been filled with both victories and challenges. As a journalist, she worked hard to build her credibility, often having to prove herself in a field dominated by men. She became a respected voice in media, yet she has spoken about moments when she felt underestimated or dismissed. But instead of backing down, she kept pushing forward. She has said, "Every time someone told me no, I used it as fuel to get better, work harder, and prove them wrong."

Maria has also been vocal about the lessons she learned from failure. She has admitted that at times, she doubted herself or questioned whether she was making a difference. But she always returned to one core belief: every setback is an opportunity to grow. She has encouraged others to embrace failure as a teacher, not as a dead end.

Her advocacy work has had its own share of challenges. Maria has fought tirelessly for Alzheimer's awareness, women's empowerment, and social justice. But she has acknowledged that making change isn't easy. She has said, "Some battles take years, even

48

decades, to win. But you don't stop fighting just because the road is long." Even when she faced resistance, she kept going because she knew the work mattered.

One of her most powerful lessons is about authenticity. Maria has spoken about the importance of being true to yourself, no matter what others expect. She has said, "For too long, I tried to be what people wanted me to be. But the real power comes from knowing who you are and standing in that truth." She encourages people, especially women, to embrace their voice, set boundaries, and never apologize for being strong.

She has also talked about the importance of kindness. Despite everything she has been through, she chooses to approach life with compassion and grace. She believes that true success isn't measured by money or titles, but by how you treat people. She has said, "At the end of the day, people won't remember your accomplishments. They'll remember how you made them feel."

Maria Shriver's life has been a mix of triumphs and setbacks, but she has never let the hard times define her. She has used every challenge as a lesson and every victory as a chance to uplift others. Her story is proof that strength comes from experience, that setbacks can lead to breakthroughs, and that life's greatest lessons come when you least expect them.

Chapter 20

A Vision for the Future

Maria Shriver has never been someone who simply looks back at her achievements and stops there. She is always focused on what's next, how she can make a difference, and what kind of world she wants to help create. She has spent years advocating for women, families, and those affected by Alzheimer's, and she is determined to keep pushing for change.

One of the biggest priorities in her vision for the future is women's empowerment. She has been clear that while progress has been made, there is still a long way to go. She wants to see more women in leadership, more women's voices being heard, and more opportunities for young girls to succeed. She has said, "Women are still being told to stay in their place, to be quiet, to not ruffle feathers. That has to end. We need to lift each other up, support one another, and fight for our space in every room where decisions are made."

Her work with The Women's Alzheimer's Movement is another key part of her future plans. Maria has been one of the strongest voices in raising awareness about how Alzheimer's disproportionately affects women. She has spoken about how the medical world has ignored this issue for too long, and she refuses to let that continue. She has said, "If we don't push for answers, who will? If we don't demand research that focuses on women, who will?" Her goal is to ensure that future generations have better prevention, treatment, and support for this devastating disease.

Maria is also deeply committed to reshaping the conversation around aging and purpose. She has talked about how society often sidelines older people, especially women, making them feel invisible. She strongly believes that aging should be seen as a new beginning, not a decline. She has said, "People ask me all the time if I'm worried about getting older. My answer is no. I'm excited. I have more wisdom, more confidence, and more to give than ever before." She wants people to embrace every stage of life with purpose and passion.

Another issue close to her heart is mental health. Maria has used her platform to encourage open conversations about anxiety, depression, and stress. She has openly shared her own struggles, saying that she has had moments of self-doubt, loneliness, and burnout. But instead of hiding it, she speaks about it because she knows others are going through the same thing. She has said, "We need to stop pretending everything is perfect. We need to start being real with each other and support each other through life's tough moments."

Maria's vision for the future isn't just about big movements and policies—it's about everyday actions. She wants people to be kinder, to listen more, and to treat one another with respect. She has said, "The world can feel overwhelming, but change starts with small steps. Be good to the people around you. Lift others up when you can. That's how we build a better future."

She has also spoken about how she wants to use her voice to encourage people to live with meaning. She believes that life isn't about chasing success, wealth, or fame—it's about finding what truly fulfills you. She has said, "I've learned that what matters most isn't what job you have or how much money you make. It's how you feel at the end of the day. It's whether you lived with integrity, whether you helped someone, whether you loved deeply."

Maria Shriver is not slowing down. She is committed to continuing her work, amplifying important issues, and inspiring people to step into their own power. She is proof that purpose doesn't fade with time—it only grows stronger. Her message is clear: The future is not just something we wait for. It's something we create, together.

Epilogue

Maria Shriver's life is a powerful example of resilience, purpose, and service. She has never settled for simply being known as a member of the Kennedy family or the former First Lady of California. Instead, she has built a legacy that stands on its own—one defined by her relentless advocacy, deep compassion, and commitment to helping others find meaning in their own lives.

Throughout her journey, Maria has spoken openly about her struggles and triumphs. She has never shied away from the truth, no matter how difficult or painful. Whether it was navigating the complexities of her public and private life, championing women's empowerment, or leading the fight against Alzheimer's disease, she has always used her voice to bring awareness to issues that matter. She has said, "I've spent my life asking questions—not just of others, but of myself. What do I stand for? What kind of impact do I want to have? How can I make a difference?"

Her work has always been about more than personal success. Maria believes that true fulfillment comes from serving others, lifting up those who feel unseen, and using one's platform to drive real change. She has dedicated years to advocating for families, mental health awareness, and education. Her efforts have helped shape policies and inspire countless individuals to take action in their own communities. "We all have a role to play," she has said. "It's not about waiting for someone else to fix things—it's about stepping up and doing what you can."

Even as she reflects on her life, Maria is far from slowing down. She continues to write, speak, and challenge people to rethink what it means to live with purpose. Her work with The Women's Alzheimer's Movement is more than just a passion project—it's a mission she has poured her heart into, pushing for more research, funding, and support for those affected by the disease. She has said, "This is not just about my family. It's about millions of families. It's about changing the future."

Maria Shriver's story is not just about personal achievement. It is about transformation, about finding meaning in every experience—whether joyful or painful—and using it to help others. She has shown that no setback is final, no challenge is insurmountable, and no voice is too small to create change. "You are not defined by your circumstances," she has reminded people time and time again. "You are defined by how you rise."

Her legacy is still unfolding, but one thing is clear—Maria Shriver has never stopped growing, questioning, and fighting for what she believes in. Her life is a testament to the idea that strength is not about having all the answers. It's about being willing to ask the right questions, to evolve, and to leave the world better than you found it.

Made in the USA
Las Vegas, NV
31 March 2025

20358041R00038